HIDDEN PIECES BUT NOW REVEALED

Johnnie G. Redmond

Unless otherwise indicated all Scripture quotations are taken from the KJV *Life in the Spirit Study Bible* by Zondervan: New edition (2003). Used by permission. All rights reserved.

Cover by POSH ANNOUNCEMENTS for Young Dreams Publications, Lansing, Illinois

Copyright ©2016 by Johnnie G. Redmond
ISBN-10: 0692757376
ISBN-13: 978-0692757376

CONTACT:
Johnnie G. Redmond
Founder/Pastor Emmanuel Temple Evangelistic Church
343 E. 115th Street, Chicago, IL 60628
www.emmanueltemple-ec.org

LCCN: Pending
STATE: Pending

All rights reserved. No part of this publication may be reproduced, stored in a retrieval system, or transmitted in any form or by any means – electronic, mechanical, digital, photocopy, recording, or any other – except for brief quotations in printed reviews, without the prior permission of the publisher.

Acknowledgements

God the Father, God the Son, God the Holy Ghost

HIDDEN PIECES BUT NOW REVEALED

IF YOU WOULD ONLY

OPEN THE BOOK AND SEE

Preface

Ephesians 3:3-5 (KJV) - How that by revelation he (God) made known unto me the mystery; (as I wrote afore in few words, whereby, when ye read, ye may understand my knowledge in the mystery of Christ). Which in other ages was not made known unto the sons of men, as it is now revealed unto his holy apostles and prophets by the Spirit.

Over my thirty-six years of being in the Lord, God has led me into the wilderness by the Holy Spirit to be tempted of the Devil. Through this temptation God has given me revelation, deep revelation, which I believe is soul saving and enlightening. I would even say that the revelation that God has given me could even appear as a commentary to be used while studying his Holy Book – which I call "Route 66 to Heaven" – also known as the Holy Bible.

In the generation we live in today it is important that we know our adversary, God's will for our lives, and how we may overcome our flesh. With this book and revelation from the Lord, I will use the guiding of the Holy Spirit to edify you. It is my prayer that you use this revelation to accomplish all these things. We can no longer afford to play with our salvation. We have to be sincere and aware of all that we must overcome.

Play time has now ended and it's time to seek the Lord like never before. These are truly praying times. Look at all the killings we're seeing right in our home cities. Police killings, we're killing one another, the love of many has waxed cold, and the drugs have truly taken over the people's lives in ways that we've never seen before.

If you are not sober and vigilant you may find yourself overtaken by the wicked one, or even worst, spiritually dead and not even know it. We must learn to be aware of the enemy's devices as well as be aware of our flesh. The only way I believe that this is achievable is to know and understand that the hidden mysteries that God left right in his Holy Word, has now been revealed.

He that has an ear, let him hear what the Spirit is saying to the church…

Chapter 1
HIDDEN PIECES

It is very common for many to open up the Word of God, read a scripture, and then it goes completely over their heads. Or you may read a scripture and it's not peculiar enough to peak your interest so you never seek revelation – you simply take it at face value.

There is one particular scripture that has intrigued me over the years and in my time in the wilderness I sought revelation from the Lord. Many never recognized the hidden revelation and hidden truth of Genesis 1:2:

"…darkness was upon the *face of the deep*. And the Spirit of God moved upon the *face of the waters*."

In order for you to understand my curiosity of this scripture allow me to take you back to the beginning. Before Adam dwelt on the earth water and darkness were the only two things covering the heavens and the earth - this same darkness on the earth was upon the face of the deep. So as I read the scripture in Genesis 1:2, "…darkness was upon the face of the deep. And the Spirit of God moved upon the face of the waters" I began to ask

God, "Why did you only move upon the face of the waters and not the face of the deep?" The Lord didn't show me right away, but I continued to seek for revelation about this matter.

Again I pondered that darkness remained on "the deep". Once more I asked the Lord, "What is the deep, and why did you leave the darkness upon it?" I believe it's a legitimate question. Surely if he was coming to bring light into the world to make it habitable for Adam, surely he should touch everything in it – even the deep, right? After time in the Word and the Spirit, the Lord began to enlighten my eyes to why he left the darkness upon the face of the deep.

God began to reveal to me that the Spirit of God didn't move upon the face of the deep because the deep was where he housed the underworld. The darkness was also upon the face of the deep because the face of the deep was a mystery. What made it a mystery is because it was, and still is, an underworld – also known as hell. It is a place where men cannot get to, but Christ can send you there. Ever wonder why man can't get to the heart of the earth? God has caused the face of the deep to be such a mystery that no matter how hard they attempt they cannot reach the core of the earth – this is assumed to be where the underworld resides. It's amazing to think that hell is so close to us, yet is so far away.

The Lord created the underworld to be hidden from the physical world – *the earthly world*. God also allowed the holy men of God to reference the underworld and what was hidden in them:

- In Luke 16:19-31, the rich man and Lazarus were alive in this world (the underworld).
- Paul said in Ephesians 4:8-9, Christ descended first into the lower parts, the deep parts of the earth or underworld, and led captivity captive (i.e. led souls that were in Abraham's bosom out of captivity).
- Peter said in 1 Pet 3:19, Christ went and preached unto the spirits in prison; or the spirits that was in the underworld.

Revelations 9:1-2 speaks about the abyss, which is the deep; also known as the underworld. The chapter states that a star came out of heaven and unlocked the bottomless pit with the key that was given him, and locusts came out. I believe that Revelations 9 is an important chapter in the Word of God to give a vast understanding about the underworld, the deep, the abyss because the locusts have a direct symbolism of the darkness and water covering the earth during the days before Adam.

Scientists, theologians, and most humans believe that before the world, as we know it today, came about that there were dinosaurs and cave man. I, too, believe that there was some other form of life prior to the creation of today; however, my belief is slightly different. I believe that the creation prior to Adam and Eve's creation was filled with creatures, spirits and dinosaur-like giants. I believe this creation also had the ability to sin. I believe that Satan was allowed to go back and forth between Heaven (or the third heavens) and this former creation. And just like the third part of the angels in heaven, I believe that Satan was able to deceive this creation. Because of that creation's sin God destroyed it with water and darkness. I believe the creatures (locusts) mentioned in Revelations 9 were the creatures that lived in that creation that was destroyed by darkness and water.

Now I know you may think of locust in your imagination and may not be able to grasp how a locust could sin against the Lord. But you have to get out of the natural and tap into the spiritual realm. Don't think of small flying insects, but think of giant creatures – almost in the sense of an alien that have the ability to think and make decisions.

The scripture in Revelations 9 goes on to say that when the fifth angel sounded these creatures (the locusts) came out of the underworld into our world and was given a commandment to torment men for five months.

So does that give you an idea of how the above statement can be true? If they were allowed to torment men for five months, is it impossible for them not to have the ability to think and make their own decisions back then? It is my belief that these creatures, *when they roamed their earth that the Lord created for them* - were deceived by Satan it was at the same time when he deceived a third part of the stars of heaven (Revelations 12:4). And I also believe these creatures and that creation are currently hid under water in the darkness that is in the water ready to be released during the great tribulation. This is why I believe the water surrounds the earth.

Now let's go back to Genesis 1:2: ...*darkness was upon the face of the deep...*

Deep[1] is defined as a deep place or any of the deepest parts, as in water or earth, the middle part; part that is darkest; that unknown; hard to understand.

- 2 Peter 2:4 says: *For if God spared not the angels that sinned, but cast them down to hell, and delivered them into chains of darkness, to be reserved unto judgment.*

- Jude 1:6 says: *And the angels which kept not their first estate, but left their own habitation, he hath reserved in everlasting chains under darkness unto the judgment of the great day.*
- Matthew 8:12 says: *But the children of the kingdom shall be cast out into outer darkness: there shall be weeping and gnashing of teeth.*
- Matthew 5:29 says: *And if thy right eye offend thee, pluck it out, and cast it from thee: for it is profitable for thee that one of thy members should perish, and not that thy whole body should be cast into hell.*

The devils in Luke 8:27 asked Christ *command us not to go into the deep.* Jesus said in Luke 16:29 *the rich man he lifted up his eyes in hell being in torment*, however, Lazarus was not in torment because he was in Abraham bosom. Abraham's bosom was considered to be lower paradise – a resting place for the believers until Jesus unlocked heaven's doors.

As we can see, the darkness of the deep was a special darkness that wasn't meant for a pleasurable experience. The darkness that was upon the face of the deep is different from the darkness that our world experiences. The darkness upon the face of the deep was a darkness of condemnation and judgment. The physical darkness of our world today is a foreshadowing of the darkness to come. However, God did allow the world to experience the darkness of the underworld twice in the scriptures in Exodus 10:21-23 and Matthew 27:45 – there is possibly a third time when you think about how God destroyed Noah's world with the flood.

Satan, his angels, and the underworld lived in the darkness of the deep the entire time before God created the world that Adam and Eve would inhabit. This deep, the underworld of the ungodly, is the eternal darkness those that die in sin will experience. Again, this darkness represents God's condemnation and judgment.

Condemn[2] means to pass judgment on; disapprove of strongly; to declare to be guilty of wrong doing; convict; to pass sentence or a penalty upon; to doom; to declare unfit for use or service.

Judgment[3] means the act of judging; deciding; sentence given by a judge; to look on as punishment from God.

The two definitions above proves why we know that Satan and his angels are casted into this darkness because they are guilty of wrong doing, and will be sentenced in the day of their judgment (Jude 1:6). This verdict is the second death which is the lake of fire that burns with fire and brimstone.

This eternal darkness was not created in, or for, Adam's world. The serpent deceived Eve, she ate of the tree, gave to her husband and he did eat (Genesis 3:6): death by sin came and entered into the world. This opened the door to eternal darkness to enter into Adam and Eve's world. This eternal darkness is Satan's world - the underworld. We should have never experienced this eternal darkness - this darkness is evil. When this door opened up, it allowed for Satan and his angels to enter into our world to make war with good – Adam and Eve were good.

The scripture says in Romans 7:21 that when I would do good, evil is present with me. This eternal darkness we should have never experienced. Why? Because this is a darkness that cannot be seen with the physical eyes, only through spiritual eyes. John 3:3, except a man be born again he cannot see... 2 Corinthians 4:4, lest the light of the glorious gospel of Christ should shine upon them...

Again, this eternal darkness should have never been experienced in our creation. Why? Because this darkness

(Satan) had experience with the light of God (2 Corinthians 11:14). Because of his experience with the light of God, he now knows how to transform himself into an angel of light to deceive the very elect, if it be possible (Matthew 24:24). And his ministers, also, transform themselves into apostles of Christ and ministers of righteousness; whose end shall be according to their works (2 Corinthians 11:13).

This darkness is full of lies and deception. This is why the Holy Scriptures, said woe unto them that call evil good, and good evil; that put darkness for light and light for darkness.

Isaiah 14:15-17 says: *Yet thou shalt be brought down to hell, to the sides of the pit. They that see thee shall narrowly look upon thee, and consider thee, saying, is this the man that made the earth tremble, that did shake kingdoms; that made the world as a wilderness…*

Most believers, and even non-believers, don't understand death because death comes from the spirit world, and the spirit world is that darkness that I've been expounding upon thus far.

Remember the tree of the knowledge of good and evil? It spoke about death, but yet death didn't come into our universe until Adam ate. This very act of disobedience is how Satan received the keys of death – the disobedience of Adam delivered hell to our lives. When Adam ate off the tree of the knowledge of good and evil, Satan received the keys of physical and spiritual death in the earth. This is how Satan got the power over death.

But by the mercies of God, he so loved the world that he gave up his only begotten Son to redeem us from the powers of death – only if you believe.

Death didn't come from God, but by Satan; however, the Lord can send death in our universe. For an example, in the days of Noah it repented the Lord that he made man and that world was destroyed by water. He also destroyed Sodom and Gomorrah with the cities roundabout with fire and brimstone. God sent an angel during King David's time and men died by an angel with the flap of his wing. And we can look in our generation today and see that death is on rampage.

Death comes by two ways – the wrath of God or the wrath of Satan. Satan is out to deceive and take the lives of the world through death – *physically and spiritually.* God sends death when his wrath becomes judgment. We all have our appointed time to experience physical death, but only those that die in the Lord shall see God. With death looming this should give the believer a zeal and a fire to make it to the new heaven and new earth, where the scripture says he shall wipe away tears from our eyes (reference Rev. 21).

But before this new heaven and new earth, just remember this, the last enemy that shall be destroyed is death.

The scriptures speak about Satan having power over death and the world. Jehovah God spoke about this death in the beginning to Adam, but Adam didn't understand "thou shalt surely die." God is not the God of the dead but the living. Satan lost his spiritual life and became the god of death.

Luke 4:6 - Jesus destroyed spiritual death through his death. And in our death (death of the flesh, ungodliness) we can destroy him (Satan and flesh). Christ received the power of heaven and earth and the keys of hell and death. Through the acceptance of Christ we then received power over the works of the flesh and the works of the Devil. We need to see Satan as being everything that the flesh is. If you can look at flesh and see Satan you can begin to call everything that God sees as evil, evil.

Let us exercise our senses to discern good and evil: the spirit of Truth and spirit of Error.

There is only one Spirit of Truth (John 14:17) and Jesus spoke of him. The Spirit of Truth came from the

Father. The scripture speaks about the God-head body: God the Father, the Son and the Holy Ghost. And Jesus said to the disciples in John 14:17 even the spirit of truth whom the world cannot receive. So if the world cannot receive the spirit of truth how can they discern the spirit of truth and the spirit of error? Jesus said the world cannot receive the spirit of truth because it see him not; neither know him. But he said to his disciples for ye know him for he dwell with you and in you.

Our senses cannot be exercised to discern good and evil if we have not been delivered from the powers of darkness which is the spirit of error. When Jesus said, "ye know him and he dwell with you" this mean you are translated into Christ's kingdom - meaning you have been born again. And Jesus said to Nicodemus that except a man be born again he cannot see the kingdom of God. So to know the spirit of truth is to be born in the kingdom of Christ. And then we can discern everything in the flesh that it cannot please God.

INTERLUDE

Another hidden revelation and hidden truth gone unnoticed is the scripture of Genesis 1:2-3:

God's spoken words are very powerful. In this very familiar scripture God speaks, *let there be light and there was light.* This strongly shows that when God is ready to do his work he can only work in His light; he cannot work in darkness. Jehovah God created our current heaven and earth in his light (Ps. 104:24). Jehovah God is not the only one that works in the light, Jesus Christ does, too. (John 9:14). If Jehovah God worked in his light to create his universe, he also worked in his light to create the believer. (Eph. 2:10).

Jehovah God created us in his image to walk after his likeness, but we can only be in his likeness while we are in Christ. Christ is the light (Col. 3:10). Christ is the light that the Father uses to do his work in the body of Christ.

The Word (Jesus) was that light that the Father used as he did his work in this universe. So many believers are not being created in Christ's image because they cannot become God's workmanship. He uses his skill to work on the heart because the heart is so deep.

What natural man on earth can spiritually reach the heart, but God? God can reach it because he knows it. He can reach it because the king's heart is in the hands of the Lord. He can reach it because he hardened Pharaoh's heart for his will. He knows the heart because he searches all hearts and understands all the imagination of our thoughts.

If the believer cannot give the Father all of their heart he cannot create them in the image of Christ. The image of Christ is what the Father created in Adam.

You may ask then, if God can reach and knows the hearts of the world why isn't everyone saved? Great question and there is an answer. Every heart belongs to the individual and it has to be a willing heart to surrender to God. God, being all knowing can see your heart. He also gives free will. If he forced everyone with manipulation to serve him then he would have nothing but robot saints. God can minister to your heart because he knows it, but the individual has to hand the heart over to God.

God couldn't change Satan's heart, nor did he try. Because of the iniquity found in Satan's heart (Eze. 28:15) God could not force a change of the haughty heart of Satan that wanted to be like the most high (Is. 14:14).

In bringing us back to God speaking light into the world, how long do you think darkness was in the heavens and earth before God said let there be light? How long do you think darkness was in the world until Jesus said I am the light of the world (John 8:12)?

While we may not know how long there was darkness upon earth before God decided to speak light into the world we do know how long it was before the *Light of the World* came into our creation. The light of Christ came after 42 generations.

Understand that when light came on earth God did not destroy darkness but divided it. He divided day from the night, made the sun to rule the day and the moon and stars to rule the night. God allowed darkness to stay because he is not the god of this world – Satan is (2 Cor. 4:4). Jesus did not come to destroy spiritual darkness in world, but to let his light rule his life in our lives when we are translated into the kingdom of God.

Without the power of Christ we cannot cast off the works of darkness and control the darkness that is in our flesh. Jesus is who Satan always wanted to be. Jesus is God's glory. God made man in his image to show Satan who he could not ever be. That's the mystery of God's creation and why he made man. God mocked Satan's sin when he forgave man and sent Jesus to be made sin for man. Satan thought he could get the whole world against God, but the few saints outweigh the sinners because in the end we're going to reign with God.

Chapter 2
THE BEGINNING OF ALL FALLS

The great fall: O, Lucifer or O, day star.

O, day star is the same as saying, O, morning star (Job 38:7). The morning stars are ordained to sing praise and worship unto the Lord. O, day star was also ordained to hold and lead this praise and worship in heaven. Before Satan became Satan, he was Lucifer in the heavenly gates of heaven.

There is a hidden revelation and hidden truth to the beginning of all falls. Imagine, if you will, anointed cherubs in heaven with the ability to make beautiful, melodic music in heaven; the most stunning, excellent worship that you could ever hear. Imagine an angel-being deck out in priceless jewels; jewels that have never been seen before that possess the most brilliant glimmer that you could visualize.

This stunning creature, in which your human imagination is possibly not even doing justice in comparison to how beautiful he actually were, was Lucifer in heaven going in and out of the presence of God. Musical instruments were created in him; anointed tabrets and pipes.

It could also be true that God named him, O, day star because of his brightness that came from this heavenly being. When you think of a star they shine, Lucifer's brightness made him the great, O, day star. I imagine that his precious stones only got even brighter when he strutted throughout heaven. Think about when you move a diamond around in the light how the different facets of the ring's clarity lights up before your eyes – Lucifer was a walking multi-precious gem.

Because God creates everything in light and in beauty, this could be the reason why he received expressed permission from God to walk up and down in the midst of the stones of fire (Ez. 28:14). This precious creature, this flawless beauty that the Creator created made the Father marvel and allows the Father to be much glorified. The brightness of Lucifer's stones released a certain radiance of exquisiteness in the midst of the stones of fire. Lucifer believed that his brightness pleased the Father more than others. Although, he was correct that his beauty pleased the Father, Lucifer allowed the praise he received to deceive him.

Praise leaded to pride and a haughty spirit became the iniquity that was found in Lucifer. From this iniquity he deceived his own self and became the father of lies. By saying in his heart, *I will ascend into heaven; I will exalt my throne above the stars of God. I will sit also upon the mount of the congregation in the sides of the north. I will ascend above the heights of the clouds. I will be like the Most High* (Is. 14:13). The third part of the angels in heaven believed Lucifer's lie and were deceived. Lucifer convinced the angels that he would be able to overthrow God in his kingdom and sit on God's throne. This dreadful lie divided heaven and war was made in heaven (Rev. 12:7).

Through God's power Lucifer, now Satan, was defeated. That liar and deceiver, along with his angels, were cast out into darkness and became the prince of darkness and over the powers of darkness.

Satan and his angels are called the power of darkness (Luke 22:53 & Col. 1:13). Some may question why would God give them so much power? Some may ask why are they the power over darkness?

They are the power of darkness because they are super natural beings – they don't operate by the same rules as human beings because they are spirits. They are darkness because they became darkness through the disobedience of sin and were casted into darkness. They made war with the Light and fell out of heaven, or fell out of the Light. And they were cast into a darkness that was in this heaven and earth - before God said let there be light.

Before we go any further you have to understand the difference between the darkness Satan was casted into versus the darkness that was upon the earth. The darkness that Satan and his angels were cast into was the darkness of the underworld. The darkness God divided from the light (Gen. 1:4) upon the earth was the darkness of judgement as result of the sin of the creation before Adam and Eve.

Satan did not become the prince of darkness that was upon the earth until Adam ate from the tree of the knowledge of good and evil. As sin entered into the world through Adam's disobedience the darkness that was divided from the light became a more evil darkness, and Satan became the prince of darkness and Adam became the works of darkness (Rom. 13:12).

This is why we know in Gen. 1:1 the judgment of God came upon the heaven and the earth with darkness and waters. And the third part of the earth is full of waters which is called the seas (Gen. 1:10). Judgment came upon

Jesus' generations with darkness (Matt. 27:45). I believe this darkness is what the heaven and the earth experienced before God said let there be light (Gen. 1:3).

This is the same darkness I believe Satan and his angels were casted into (Rev. 12:9). Remember Jesus said the children of the kingdom shall be cast out into outer darkness (Matt. 8:12)? This is that eternal darkness that is separate from the physical darkness that we see now. When Jehovah God said let there be light this eternal darkness could not have any part of Adam and Eve's creation – it had to be separated because it became a spiritual darkness for eternal judgement. Before Adam and Eve sinned they knew nothing about this eternal judgement. They were perfect creatures. There was no need for them to feel or sense this eternal darkness that was judgement.

However, when Adam and Eve ate off the tree of the knowledge of good and evil the spiritual door was opened to this physical world which gave access to Satan and his angels to reside within the earth with this eternal darkness. Man would then taste this darkness and live forever in everlasting spiritual darkness with Satan and his angels. For Jesus did say men loved darkness rather than light (John 3:19; Rev. 20:10; 15; and Matt. 25:41-46).

This is why Paul says let us cast off the work of darkness that will send us into everlasting darkness, but put on the armor of light that will keep us in everlasting light, which is the presence of the Lord (Rom. 13:12).

You must remember that God is Light, like the day light, sun, moon, lightings (Rev. 21:23). God is light and in him is no darkness at all (1 John 1:5). With God the city had no need of the sun, neither of the moon, to shine in it. For the glory of God did lighten it and the Lamb is the light thereof (Rev. 21:23).

Although there was a physical light upon the earth, once sin came into this world the spiritual Light was hidden from man. The Light was available to man, but there was only one way to access it. The sun and moon is a foreshadowing of two spiritual lights from God. Remember in Gen. 1:16 God made two great lights; the greater light to rule the day and the lesser light to rule the night.

The Light that comes from the law of God is the lesser light – not less important – but is lesser because you cannot see nor understand this Light with your physical eye. You must be alive spiritually to see and understand.

We could not become spiritually alive until Jesus came; this is why I believe Jesus said I am the Light of the world – meaning being a greater Light. Jesus became that greater Light to quicken our dead spirits and to rule his life that would dwell in us through repentance and acceptance of him.

The law of God is the lesser light to rule and discern the spirits that come to deceive us (1 John 4:1). When the Light of his Life is ruling within us we won't be deceived by the spirits of this world and the ungodly spirits in the churches. Many of us are unaware of the spirits that rule within this world. If you're in your Word and studying to show yourself approved you would understand and know these spirits. What spirits don't you know by now? Here are a few you should know:

- Rev. 16:14 – The spirits of devils working miracles.
- Matt. 24:24 – False prophets that if it were possible they shall deceive the very elect. Prophesying, having the word of knowledge, gifts of healing, working miracles, interpretation of tongues.
- 1 Cor. 12:11 – Spirits working that one and the selfsame Spirit, dividing every man severally as he will.
- Rom. 12:3 According as God has dealt to every man the measure of faith. Having then gifts

differing according to the grace that is given to us whether it be prophecy, let us prophesy according to the proportion of faith.

If you're a child of God you should know these spirits. Most importantly if you profess to be a minister of God you should definitely know these spirits. Have you been tried in the wilderness to know and understand how these spirits operate? Ministers of God, how much experience do you have in the word of righteousness? How much experience do you have in ministry? It is important that we wait on our ministering because many that teach on teaching actually need to be taught themselves. (Rom. 12:7).

Being well-versed in the scriptures coupled with the endowing of the Holy Spirit gives you revelation and experience with the powers of darkness and how they operate. Being a child of God is more than blessings and prosperity. You must be aware of Satan and his ultimate plan for those who don't know God. This is the power of eternal darkness:

- Eternal darkness blinds the minds of people
- Controls with the powers of lust
- Deceives with their lies
- They shew great signs and wonders because they transform themselves to an angel of light

- They understand the darkness
- They are full of filthiness and uncleanness of the flesh

God has given us plenty of space to escape eternal darkness through his Word and the power of Jesus. I believe that part of the judgement of hell is that God has allowed those condemned to hell to see Satan. I believe that the unveiling of Satan for their physical eye is a portion of their torment. Remember the saying, "I told you so"? The saying that people say when they tried to warn you of something but you refused to listen, then when your plans blow up in your face that person that originally tried to warn you says, "I told you so." Even in earthly situation, there's a level of torment of wishing we would have listened when someone tried to warn us. Therefore, you can imagine that the torment of those in hell is magnified on a greater scale upon the revelation that Satan is real and that God's Word is true.

Satan and his angels live in darkness. The darkness that they abide in is a state of condemnation and judgment – meaning that they have been judged already. When God judges the world at the last day, Satan and his angels do not have to be sentenced because they have already been sentenced. They are aware that upon judgement day they will be sent to their final resting place of the lake of fire.

Everything upon the earth, the heavens, and the underworld is waiting for the judgement of God. Heaven is even on lock down and waiting to be recreated. The heaven that Lucifer resided in before he became Satan is no longer accessible.

The beginning of all falls is when Satan became everything that the flesh is. In order to understand flesh you must understand who Satan is. He possesses that high thing that desires to be lifted up. When Satan saw Jehovah God, he saw God high and lifted up (Is. 14:13) – Satan didn't understand that he needed to cast down imaginations, and every high thing that exalteth itself against the knowledge of God and bringing into captivity every thought to the obedience of Christ (2 Cor. 10:5).

Satan became exalted: not knowing that whosoever shall exalt himself shall be abased and he that shall humble himself shall be exalted (Matt. 23:12).

He became prideful: not knowing that pride goeth before destruction (Prov. 16:18).

He became a haughty spirit: not knowing that an haughty spirit comes before a fall (Prov. 16:18).

He became sin: not knowing that all unrighteousness is sin (1 John 5:17).

He became death: the good that was in O, Lucifer died in him. Iniquity appeared and that iniquity worked spiritual death in him and he became all that the flesh is.

He that hath an ear let him hear what the Spirit says unto the church (Rev. 2:11).

Satan became all that flesh is. The character of Satan dwelled in the tree of the knowledge of good and evil. What Adam ate he became! The tree of the knowledge of good and evil put him under the law of sin and death. David reminds us that in Psalm 51:5 we were shaped in iniquity and in sin did our mothers conceive us. Because of the sin of Adam we're automatically born into sin; we become a different type of flesh - flesh that is full of sin; flesh that possesses the character of Satan.

Satan is darkness and darkness is evil, and if darkness exists in you it will control that evil. Darkness is a blindness that will blind the mind and eyes; it will blind you to a state where you cannot understand and receive knowledge and choose the fear of the Lord. Darkness, first, became a darkness of judgement: then a spiritual darkness: then a worldly darkness: then an eternal darkness: then an outer darkness: then chains of darkness: then you became trapped under darkness that you cannot receive the love of the truth to be saved from the darkness that bounds you in ignorance: then darkness became torment: darkness can give you a taste of hell, darkness can put you in captivity.

Now, one may ponder, "If God never gave Satan the freedom to possess the serpent then sin would have never entered into our world. Why was Satan the only creature of the underworld given the freedom to enter into Adam and Eve's world through the serpent?"

Take the following scriptures into consideration:

- Ezekiel 28:14: *Thou art the anointed cherub that covereth; and I have set thee so: thou was upon the holy mountain of God; thou hast walked up and down in the midst of the stones of fire.*
- Job 1:6-7: *Now there was a day when the sons of God came to present themselves before the Lord, and Satan came also among them. And the Lord said unto Satan, Whence comest thou? Then Satan answered* the Lord, and said, From going to and fro in the earth, and from walking up and down in it.

- Matthew 12:43: *When the unclean spirit is gone out of a man, he walketh through dry places, seeking rest, and findeth none.*
- 1 Peter 5:8: *Be sober, be vigilant; because your adversary the Devil, as a roaring lion, walketh about, seeking whom he may devour.*

As you can see Satan had, and has, much freedom to roam. I remember, as I ministered this teaching to my congregation, one member asked (reflecting back on the world that was before Adam and Eve's world), "So did Satan have permission to walk in the creation before Adam and Eve's world?"

To which I responded, "Yes."

Then they asked, "What was his purpose for walking in the creation?"

I believe the answer to this question is: He was one of the eyes of the Lord to report everything he saw. I believe God uses angels as his eyes. The Word says in Genesis 18:20-23, that the Lord said because the cry of Sodom and Gomorrah was great and because their sin was very grievous, that he went down hastily to see whether they had done altogether according to the cry of it, which had come unto him; and if it did he would know it. He also referenced this in Proverbs 15:3: The eyes of the Lord are in every place, beholding the evil and the good.

Of course we know that the Lord did get off his throne and go to Sodom and Gomorrah himself but sent two angels (Gen. 19:1). Again, as you can see, Satan had, and has, much freedom to roam. Satan even said himself, (Is. 14:14) I will ascend above the heights of the clouds. I will ascend into heaven. I will be like the Most High.

This high-minded thinking was the lust that was created in his heart. You may ask how I may know this. Go back to read Isaiah 14:13 says it's declare that he said it in his heart. Lust deceived Satan; he and the angels were already like God in terms of being a spiritual beings and being flames of fire (Heb. 1:7; Heb. 12:29; and John 4:24).

Again, referencing the four scriptures I previously quoted from Ezekiel, Job, Matthew, and 1 Peter, Satan had much liberty to roam. Scripture is clear that Satan, who Lucifer, was one of a small, select few that had permission to come in and out of God's presence.

It is my belief that as Satan traveled throughout the earth and heavens after his fall he finally acknowledged within himself that he could not be God – he realized he was under God's feet. The scriptures said that heaven was the Lord's throne and the earth was his footstool. The only authority Satan knew he possessed was to rule the dark world and over those that were like him in the natural world, as the scriptures says that he that practices sin is of the Devil. Jesus also said that ye are like your father, the Devil, and the lust of your father ye will do (Acts 7:49; 1 John 3:9; John 8:44).

The authority that Satan owns he hides from the unbeliever to control their minds, bodies, and affections. But to the believer, Paul said we are not ignorant of Satan's devices (1 Cor. 2:11). With Satan having this knowledge, within his heart he believes he can rule the world because of the advantage he had in the dark world, which is our world. He understands that his presence is not greater than the Lord's; therefore, he fights the believer to keep them out of the Lord's presence. Satan knows that in the presence of the Lord there is fullness of joy. David said cast me not away from thy presence.

Which brings us back to, "Is this the man?" (Isaiah 14:16). *Is this the man that made the earth tremble, that did shake kingdoms; that made the world as a wilderness...*

Chapter 3
TREE OF THE KNOWLEDGE OF GOOD AND EVIL

As we understand from the previous chapters, we know that darkness entered into this universe through the tree of the knowledge of good and evil. This is the second fall - Satan was the beginning of all falls, and Adam became the second fall. The devastation that Adam caused to come upon earth through his disobedience was never a part of God's plan. God never wanted man to experience the darkness of sin. The Lord God commanded the man saying that he could freely eat of every tree but the tree of the knowledge of good and evil. Even in putting the tree in the garden we recognized that God always gave man free will and also helps us to understand how spiritual death became a part of our lives.

Adam was alive spiritually in the Garden of Eden. He had a connection with God and was right with God. But unfortunately Adam ended up experiencing two of the three major deaths after sin approached – physical and spiritual death. Not only did Adam experience spiritual death, but he also experienced darkness. The darkness he experienced was being separated from God and losing the closeness that he once knew in God. One form of darkness he experienced was loss of his son, Abel, by the hands of his son, Cain.

Darkness and death abide in one another; you can't have one without the other. Death also comes in three stages: spiritual death, physical death; and eternal death (it is my belief that Adam was able to escape eternal death). Man, upon entering this world through birth by a woman, will experience spiritual and physical death; but can also escape eternal death through Jesus. Jesus came to redeem us from all three deaths.

However, I find it amazing that the saints today are not aware of, nor have the understanding of these deaths that walk with us every day.

What is spiritual death?

Spiritual death is the separation from God when you become dead in trespass and sins. Spiritually, God is not the God of the dead, but the God of the living (Matt. 22:32). Christ came to redeem the inner man and restore him back to God. The first death that every man will experience is the death of the spirit that resides in man's body. The Bible states that God must quicken us (Eph. 2:1) from within to make us alive. If our souls are not quickened (awake) then we remain sinners and have no peace with God. God breathed into man and made him a living soul – the body is just a covering but it is the soul that lives and dies (Matt. 10:28).

What is physical death?

Physical death is the death of the body – the physical form. The Garden of Eden was originally a paradise - the place where human beings were going to reign on earth forever. Adam and Eve and the creation that was birth through them were supposed to live forever. Their physical man was to never experience corruption, immortality, destruction, or decay. Upon Adam's disobedience he was only allowed to live 930 years; his disobedience lead to the corruption, immortality, destruction and decay of his physical body. But grace be to God and because of the love he has for his creation, those that die in the Lord, God will resurrect their bodies at the last day. The body that he created will be redeemed because everything he made was good. And with this revelation this is why I teach against cremation – your body is not your body to destroy. The body naturally turns into dust and ashes - why rush something that will naturally happen on its own and is a part of God's plan.

What is eternal death?

Eternal death is being separated from eternal life throughout eternity. Eternal life is only given by Jesus Christ. In Luke 16:19 the Bible speaks on eternal death when the rich man lifted up his eyes in hell being in torment, but yet alive. This eternal death is the first death of eternity; the second death is at the final judgement. Eternal death is when the ungodly will be casted into the lake of fire that burns with fire and brimstone. When you experience the first death this is when your physical man returns to the dust and your spirit man goes into eternity. In the final death God will resurrect your body and cast it into the lake of fire for eternal torment. We must understand that God's original plan for man during earthly paradise (Garden of Eden) was not for us to experience death because God is the God of the living.

Eve also ate of the tree of the knowledge of good and evil. The Word of God states that she was in transgression but not Adam (1 Tim. 2:14). Many ask the question of why did she eat? The answer remains in the scripture - the serpent beguiled her by awakening the lust of eye, lust of the flesh and the pride of life within her. The serpent taunted her with the words, "for God do know that in the day you eat thereof, your eyes will be open and you will be as gods knowing good and evil" (Gen. 3:5).

Eve didn't know that when Satan said, "you will be as gods", that Satan was revealing that a door would be open to fight against good and evil. Eve didn't know that Satan was setting her up to, not only cause Adam to bring sin into the world, but they would have the knowledge of knowing that God was good and Satan was evil, and a choice to live righteous or as a sinner would be available.

Hebrew 5:14 - But strong meat belongs to them that are of full age, even those who by reason of use have their senses exercised to discern both good and evil.

Isaiah 5:20 - Woe unto them that call evil good and good evil that put darkness for light and light for darkness that put bitter for sweet and sweet for bitter.

Deuteronomy 30:15 - See I have set before thee this day life and death, and good and evil, blessings and cursings.

The scriptures above illustrate what were set before Adam and Eve. And the darkness that's in this world has blinded the minds of them that don't believe this, less the light of the glorious gospel of Christ, who is the image of God should shine upon them (2 Cor. 4:4).

But we have to understand the grace of God and his thoughts toward man. The Lord always remained mindful of Adam and continued to visit him. God knew that he would bring grace and truth through his son, Jesus. God was still a just God and dealt with Adam's disobedience by executing judgement and putting him and Eve out of the garden; but the physical and spiritual darkness did not stop the Lord from looking upon his creation.

However, sin causes us to be fearful when God visits us upon earth. Adam is the perfect example of how we fear God when he visits us when we are in our sins. The same light that was in Christ when he was upon the earth, is the same light that came out of heaven which caused Adam to hide himself from God (the voice of God) when he saw it.

It is truly amazing the level of cunningness and craftiness that Satan possesses. Satan is the father of lies and the god of this world; he knows the earthly realm and understands how to stimulate the lust of the flesh, lust of the eye, and pride of life that is within us. Because of the permission that he was granted to walk up and down, and to and fro throughout the earth, he's learned our weaknesses and the behavior of man.

You may ask when Satan got permission to tempt the world and possess the serpent. Once the tree of the knowledge of good and evil was put in the garden, then God let Satan out from the underworld – this is my belief.

In my time of studying I believe that the Lord showed me the revelation of and the interpretation of what Satan was saying when he spoke to Eve. There was urgency within Satan to do whatever and say whatever he could to get Eve to be so enticed through lust to eat from the tree of the knowledge of good and evil.

Imagine this conversation of Satan from Genesis 3:5:

"For God do know that in the day you eat thereof..." **(Satan's truth behind those words)** *Eve, you don't want to miss this day, don't let this day pass you by, you must eat now.*

The scripture says that he (Satan) comes immediately to bring doubt upon and take away from what the Lord has spoken unto you in efforts to have you believe the lies that he is speaking – remember, Satan is the father of lies and a thief.

"Ye shall be as gods..." **(Satan's truth behind those words)** *Your eyes will open up but your understanding will be of darkness.*

This very deception is why we have the spirit of error, divination, false spirits, Satan's angels that transform themselves into angels of light, false apostles, prophets, pastors, and teachers; these are trying to be like God, thinking they understand the ways of the Lord. They believe they understand God but have no knowledge of the depth of the riches (Rom. 11:33) of his knowledge. They believe they understand him but fail to realize that there is no searching of his understanding (Is. 40:28).

"Ye shall be gods..." **(Satan's truth behind those words)** *You can become liberated from God. You will be free to make your own choices.*

The deception of this is that Satan wanted man to believe that God was controlling them falsely. He wanted man to believe that they could have the same abilities and understanding as God did. Satan wanted them to believe in a false power.

When Adam was first created he knew God and had the mind of God because he was created in the image of God and walked in his likeness. Eating from the tree of the knowledge of good and evil walked Adam into darkness and it separated him from God. Adam would soon realize that God is light and there is no darkness in him at all.

While, yes, men did become gods, it wasn't the glorified god that Satan made it out to be. In John 10:34, the Word confirms that we are gods, "Is it not written in your law, I said, ye are gods?" There is a part in men that believes we can be God. We believe this lie when we receive glory, honor, and power upon the earth. However, man must always remember that his power on earth is false and temporal.

"Knowing good and evil…" **(Satan's truth behind those words)** *You will become like me doing only evil. You will want to do good but the evil shall overpower you* (Rom. 7:21).

Satan could not outright say the full intentions of his thoughts; therefore he had to word his words in a way that it caused doubt upon the Word of God. Satan was successful in getting Eve to believe that God was holding something good back from her.

Upon the fall of Adam, God, too, made a new revelation of what happened to man when he spoke upon it in Genesis 3:22:

> **And the Lord God said, Behold, the man is become as one of us, knowing good and evil: and now, lest he put forth his hand, and take also of the tree of life, and eat, and live for ever:**

God acknowledged that Adam and Even had now become *"as one of us…"* meaning they had now become who Satan used to be, but also now aware of good and evil. Remember Satan was originally O, Lucifer, the anointed cherub, O, day star. His beauty was in his precious stones that were created in him; this was the brightness that overshadowed him. O, Lucifer did experience the holiness of God because he was upon the Holy mountain of God, walked up and down in it and in the mist of the stone of the fire. (Ez. 28:14).

God's throne dwells in a cloud; the cloud is there to protect God's glory and holiness from the angels and the world. This is why he sits in the sides of the north upon a high mountain in the heavenly. Upon this high mountain is the holiness of all. Why is this mountain lifted up high in the heavens? It sits up high because of how holy it is - if you touch it you will die. Jehovah God is sitting high and covered in and with stones of fire upon his holy mountain. This is why he is called the Most High because he is high and lifted up. Not because the angels and the creation lift him up, but because he is exalted above all things.

God acknowledged that Adam and Eve were now able *"to know good..."* meaning they now had the ability to recognize a difference between good and evil. They now see God as good; they understand that all Jehovah God knows is good. This is hard for some to believe, but God never saw evil come before it came. Because God is holy and everything he made was good, he never knew that

Lucifer would become Satan. If God knew that I believe he would have never created Satan.

God acknowledged that Adam and Eve also came into the understanding *"to know evil..."* meaning they now have a sense of sin and ungodliness. Satan is created in evil by his own deception and man is born into evil by sin entering into the world by one man.

God was now, again, forced to make changes in his paradise. Just as God casted Satan out of heaven, Adam and Eve were forced to leave the garden. Man would not easily have access to life, *"lest he put forth his hands."* God didn't want man's hands, now wicked and unclean, on the things of God any longer. God didn't want man "t*aking also of the tree of life"* and eating from the Lord's table with filthy hands. Man no longer had the option to *"live forever."* God did not want evil to dwell in his presence again.

Now can you see the great war against good and evil? And this is a battle that we cannot fight on our own because it's spiritual. We need help from God through Christ. God was disappointed in the man that Adam became (Gen. 3:22). Adam had no idea of his identity; he didn't know who he looked like. God's image that was created in the beginning was removed from Adam. He took on the form of someone else's; he walked like another god

- Satan. Adam being naked and hiding himself was a symbolism of the garments of holiness and the robe of righteousness being removed from his divine being – the Lord had casted him away his presence.

This is why in the scriptures God wants us to put on the new man, the man Adam was before he sinned. God wants us to put on the new man that is renewed in knowledge after the image of him that created him (Col. 3:10); He wants us to put on the image of Christ, which is the new image.

We have to remember that he that commits sin is of the Devil (1 John 3:8). Because of the sin of man God can no longer be our heavenly Father. We are of our father the Devil and the Word says that the lust of your father we will do (John 8:44) when we walk in uncleanness.

God wanted the tree of the knowledge of good and evil to remain a mystery. He believed the hidden truth, secret things, and the knowledge of it could be withheld from man if he only chose to obey the voice of God. God warned man that he *"should not eat of it."* God knew that the day he ate of it that man would become it. God knew that whatever man sowed, or ate, unto his flesh shall of the flesh reap corruption (Gal. 6:8).

God knew that *"for in the day"* that man would lose his right standing before God. He wanted man to see the fear of that day coming. God wanted man to hear his voice and harden not his heart (Heb. 4:7). God never wanted man to *"surely die"*, he didn't want death to be revealed to man, but because of sin there was no other choice as his Word doesn't come back void.

"For God do know" but he never wanted man to know the knowledge of good and evil. This spiritual revelation that man finds himself in is too hard for him. In man's finite understanding God knows that man only knoweth the things of a man through the spirit that is in man; but God understands that man doesn't know the things of God, but only the Spirit of God (1 Cor. 2:11). So what is God saying? He is saying that now that you've come into the knowledge of good and evil you must find a way to gain the Spirit of God that you may know the things of God.

Therefore, by now we should have a clear understanding that the tree of the knowledge of good and evil was produced by Satan. Man, indeed, became as gods knowing good and evil. Satan understands good but, yet, he is evil; our flesh is good but, yet, does evil (John 8:44). Satan abides not in the truth because there's no truth in him (2 Cor. 11:14).

It is amazing that Satan can't abide in the truth, but yet he knows the truth. It is impossible for Satan to live in the truth of God. Because his habitation was once inside the pearly gates and the everlasting doors he has an advantage over man. This knowledge and freedom of heaven is what he is trying to keep from the believer. Satan understands that upon his casting out that heaven has since become on lockdown – not only to the spiritual world but also to the physical world. Satan's sole purpose is ensuring that man doesn't make it to heaven. He does not want man to experience what he once had when he was right with God. Satan will never give you truth, he is incapable of doing so.

Through the tree of the knowledge of good and evil Satan became the god of this world. In the beginning of all falls Lucifer desired to be like Christ. Although he didn't know the plan of Christ yet, his motives were to be just like Christ, meaning he wanted to be praise and exalted above all. Sitting on the right hand of the Father was not good enough for him; Lucifer wanted to sit on the Father's throne. When you continuously eat from the tree of the knowledge of good and evil you become just like Lucifer, you fall from grace, and you possess these characteristics:

- Lucifer desired to be everything that Christ is – but not in a good way. Lucifer wanted to be exalted while Christ humbled himself.
- Lucifer wanted to be like God, but Jesus is God and the Word was God – therefore Lucifer could never be God, God may only abide in you.
- Lucifer wanted to sit on God's throne, but Jesus sits on God's throne. He also overcame and is set down with the Father in his throne. Jesus' purpose was never to gain those things; he only wanted to do the will of the Father. Because of his obedience God gave those things to him.
- Lucifer desired all angels to worship him, but Jesus and all the angels did worship God. Let all the angels of God worship him.
- Lucifer desired to sit on the Father's throne and desired heaven and earth to become his footstool. However, he wasn't worthy of the calling.
- Lucifer exalted himself and said he will exalt his throne above the stars of God. But Jesus, when he was raised from the dead, God sat him at his own right hand in the heavenly places, far above all principality and powers and might and dominion and every name that is named.

- Lucifer desired to be like the Most High. He said I will ascend above the heights of the clouds; I will be like the Most High. But Jesus is who they shall see; the Son of Man coming in the clouds of heaven, Alpha and Omega, the beginning and the ending, the first and the last, the almighty, he is like God, the mighty God, the everlasting Father, the prince of peace, making himself equal with God, being in the form of God, thought it not robbery to be equal with God.

You will never be who God wants you to be without acknowledging the Savior and the Redeemer. God desires that Christ abide in you and not you exalt yourself above Christ. When you walk in the flesh you are exalting yourself above Christ.

Chapter 4
HEAVEN WAS ON LOCKDOWN

In thinking about the destruction that Satan caused in heaven, and now on earth, one may ask is the pearly gates and everlasting doors on lockdown? And if they are, how long have they been locked?

The answer to this question is, yes, heaven is on lockdown and has been since the beginning of the creation of Adam. One may ask, why? The answer to this question is because flesh and blood cannot inherit the kingdom of God (1 Cor. 15:50). When God created Adam he created him to be of the earth, earthly and born in the image of the earthly. The flesh that God created in man was never equipped to dwell in the heavenly realm… but also wasn't equipped to dwell in the underworld, either. With heaven being on lockdown, God gave us hope in the book of Psalms that the doors to heaven will once again be opened.

David wrote in Psalm 24:7, "Lift up your heads, O, ye gates." By inspiration from God, David was prophesying to the children of Israel to look and see who was coming. The gates represented the twelve angels that stood at the twelve gates in heaven (Rev. 21:12). David goes on to say in verse 7, "And be ye lifted up ye everlasting doors," which he's saying that the doors will open. David was prophesying that the *King of Glory* (who is Jesus) was coming. Jesus had become the door, and no man would enter into heaven but by him.

The gates and everlasting doors of heaven were on lockdown because of the war in heaven. Because of sin God had to shut the door until Jesus fulfilled the will of the Father. Jesus confirmed that heaven was on lockdown in John 3:13 when he said, "No man hath ascended up to heaven, but he that came down from heaven."

Christ was the key to open the door (John 1:51); Christ opened up the spiritual doors of heaven for mankind. We know that heaven was open to the angels that had not sinned against God because reading the Old Testament we know that the angels descended and ascended from heaven into the earthly realm because of their assignments appointed to them on earth. There are many examples in the Bible in how they ascended and descended to and from heaven to earth to do God's will. God's will had to be done on earth even as it was done in heaven before Adam sinned (Gen. 3:24), and he used angels to carry out his plan.

Examples of angels descending from heaven to do God's will:
- The Lord placed cherubim at the east of the garden to keep the way of the tree of life with a flaming sword (Gen. 3:24).
- The three angels that appeared to Abraham (Gen. 18:2).
- The two angels that appeared to Lot (Gen. 19:1).
- The angel that was sent to deliver the understanding of the vision to Daniel, and Michael (one of the chief princes) helped the angel deliver the will of God (Dan. 10:12-14).

So, again, we see why Jesus was very important to man to be able to, not only, enter into God's literal kingdom, but we needed Jesus so that we could enter into God's spiritual kingdom. Jesus is the hope for the gates that David speaks about in Psalm 24. In order to understand even further why Jesus is the hope for the gates you must understand the keys that Jesus had obtained that allowed for the unlocking of heaven.

Because Christ did the will of the Father he was able to obtain authority over hell's gates (Rev. 1:18); hell's gates are equal to the graves (John 5:28-29). Christ has the keys of hell and of death, the graves, and physical life. Christ stated in John 11:25, "I am the resurrection and the life". To understand how important it is for Christ to have the keys of hell, you must understand the meaning of the hell.

Hell is broken up into three words:
- *Gehenna*: Greek meaning the place of punishment.
- *Hades*: Greek meaning the abode of the dead.
- *Sheol*: Hebrew meaning the grave.

When Jesus gave his life for the sake of man (John 10:18) he showed his authority over hell and death. Death was swallowed up in the victory of the cross. "O death, where is thy sting? O grave, where is thy victory" (1 Cor. 15:54-56)?

It's amazing to see that, according to John 10:18, the scripture proves that Jesus had the authority over death well before he obtained the keys - death didn't have power over him, he laid down his own life. The Old Testament also shows that Jesus had authority over death. In Job 1:11-12, Satan asked the Lord to put forth his hand on Job to destroy all he had. The Lord answered Satan and told him that Job was in thou hands but to save his life. This reveals that Satan had the authority to take life, but Satan had to get permission for the lives of those that were protected by God. Before a person dies death brings fear but Jesus came to destroy him. Jesus came to destroy the Devil who used to have some, not all, power over death. Most people don't understand death because death comes from the spirit world, and the spirit world is that darkness that we've been talking about.

Remember the tree of the knowledge of good and evil? It spoke about death, but yet death didn't come into our universe until Adam ate. This is how Satan received the keys of death because Adam delivered it to him. The Devil foolishly told Christ in Luke 4:6, "all this power will I give thee, and the glory of them: for that is delivered unto me; and to whomsoever I will I give it."

Many people that received power and glory don't realize where it comes from. According to the scriptures the Lord doesn't give man power and glory at the same time. This will exalt self. The Lord choses to crown man with glory and honor – there's a difference. The scripture in Matthew 23:12 says, "Whosoever shall exalt himself shall be abased; and he that shall humble himself shall be exalted."

This is the understanding of God's power and glory:
- **Power** is God's Authority.
- **Glory** is God's presence.

This is the understanding of God's glory and honor:
- **Glory** is God's presence.
- **Honor** is to honor who he is.

God didn't give Adam power, he gave him dominion over the works of his hand. This is the reason why God doesn't give glory and power at the same time – man can't handle having authority (power) and the presence of God (glory). They become like Satan and get lifted up in what God created in them. They forget where they came from and who holds all the true power. Therefore, God keeps us humble by only giving us glory and honor. He wants up to remain in a place of humbleness. God wants us to dwell in his presence while continuing to honor who he is – he doesn't want us to dwell in his presence and believe we have authority. You cannot have authority in the presence of God.

So bringing us back to death because God so loved the world he gave us his only begotten Son to redeem us from the powers of death – only if you believe. Again, to reiterate, death didn't come from God, but the Lord can send death in our universe. There are several example of when God sent death:

- In the days of Noah, it repented the Lord that he made man and that world was destroyed by water (Gen. 6:6).
- He also destroyed Sodom and Gomorrah with the cities roundabout with fire and brimstone (Gen. 19:24).
- And sent an angel during King David's time and men died by an angel with the flap of his wing.

We can look in our generation and see death on rampage. Seeing death widespread across our world should give the believer a zeal and a fire to be more conscious about being worthy to make it to the new heaven and new earth. The scripture says God shall wipe away tears from our eyes (Rev. 21:4). But before this new heaven and new earth, just remember this, the last enemy that shall be destroyed is death. Death still exists because Jesus has not returned to give the believer everlasting life.

But until he returns, God has equipped us with a little book that provides the answers and the way to gain the keys to eternal life that Jesus possesses.

Chapter 5
THE LITTLE BOOK

Many never recognized the hidden pieces of this little book (The Holy Bible). This book is little on the outside but holds big and great things on the inside. John saw in the right hand of him that sat on the throne a book written within and on the backside, sealed with seven seals (Rev. 5:1). Revelations holds all the hidden pieces of the many mysteries and prophecies in the Bible. Revelations is the last book of the Holy Bible. Revelation is the sixty-sixth book that no man was worthy to open and to read (Rev. 5:2). Christ was the only one with the authority to open this book. Why? Because it was sealed. The mystery of all scripture, just like the book of Revelations, is sealed to the natural man. It takes Jesus to open the books spiritually so that the believer can understand. Even the apostles and people during Jesus' time didn't fully comprehend that the scriptures were a mystery about Christ (Luke 24:27).

Revelations 10:9-10 also shows that it takes the revelation and power of God for you to understand the scriptures. Apostle John was not able to prophesy the things of the scriptures, the little book, until he ate of it. Only through Jesus can you eat of the scriptures and understand them.

The little book: little on the outside but great and astonishing things on the inside. The little book: when you open and read it to look thereon it possesses the words of eternal life (John 6:68); the engrafted word which is able to save your soul (James 1:21). The little book: full of the incorruptible seed which lives and abides forever (1 Pet. 1:23), the hidden treasure in earthly vessels (2 Cor. 4:7), the Word of God which is quick and powerful and sharper than a two edged sword Heb. 4:12).

God is the author of all things in the universe. Man believes he discovers things; but God only reveals in his time. God is the author of science, biology, and math. Man didn't discover these subjects, God created it.

The little book gives man a science lesson. The definition of science[1] is to know, to discern, to distinguish the state or facts of knowledge. Experimentation carried on in order to determine the nature or principle of what is being studied.

Books of Science: a virgin conceived whose name was Mary. The Holy Ghost came upon her and the power of the highest came upon her, overshadowed her and she was impregnated with that Holy Thing whom is called the Son of God (Luke chapters 1 and 2).

The little book gives man a biology lesson. The definition of biology[2] is the science that deals with the origin or history, physical characteristics, habits of the living as plants and animals.

Book of biology: The first operation in the Lord's creation was upon Adam. He put a deep sleep upon Adam and took of his rib to make woman and closed him back up (Gen. 2:21).

Book of biology: the Lord opened the mouth of the ass to say unto Balaam what have I done unto thee that thou have smitten me these three times (Num. 22:28).

Book of biology: Jesus said unto Peter I tell thee that the cock shall not crow three times (Matt. 26:34).

Book of biology: John saw three unclean spirits coming out of the mouth of the beast working miracles (Rev. 16:12-14).

Also a book of medicine: Moses made a serpent of brass and it came to pass if the serpent bites any man when he beheld the serpent of brass he lived (Num. 21:9).

The little book is a math book. We know that two plus two equals four, but one plus two makes three - the Father, the Son, and the Holy Ghost and these are three that bear record in heaven. But this equation becomes slightly complicated because one plus three actually equals one. Only a degree in the Holy Spirit can reveal that the answer is true and right - the Father, the Word, and the Holy Ghost and these are one (1 John 5:7).

Book of math: His word created the heaven and earth in six days and the seventh day he rested (Gen. 2:2).

Book of math: The unfaithful servant that doesn't know his math in the little book will be destroyed for the word declares that the people perish for the lack of knowledge (Hos. 4:6). If man doesn't know his math he's going to die once; for it is appointed unto men once to die but after that come judgment (Heb. 9:27).

Little book gives a history lesson. The definition of history[3] is what has happened in the life or development of a people, country, and institution. Old Testament: law, history, poetry, major prophets and minor prophets. New Testament: Gospel, history, Paul's letters, general letters and prophecy.

The book written that was sealed in Jesus' hand in Revelations. God has revealed to me secret things concerning the scriptures and things that happened before this creation. God never intended for the hidden things to remain hidden, but to be revealed at an appointed time.

God never expected man to figure out on his own how to get to heaven. He provided a way to life with instructions using the Word of God. There is a purpose for the Bible, but it's up to man to find the purpose and use it properly. God warns that man will be inexcusable (Rom. 2:1).

How are the saints supposed to use the Bible? To build up their spiritual man and to overcome Satan's army and the deception that is in the world. One of Satan's tactics is to get people to question the authenticity and the writers of the Bible. But true saints of God are supposed to be able to look beyond the deception of Satan.

Saints are supposed to be able to discern the spirit of truth and error (1 John 4:6). However, if you don't study the book you'll never know the difference between truth and error. Know that the fullness of Satan's power is being held back for an appointed time; but know there will be a time to come and Satan shall be loosed (Rev. 20:7).

Christ is our high priest who went to the heavens to appear in the presence of God for us. You tell me? How shall we escape if we neglect so great a salvation – after this Christ was glorified (Luke 24:38).

Chapter 6
JESUS THE BEGINNING OF THE CREATION

Jesus Christ, the beginning of the creation of God (Col. 1:15). This is a mystery and a secret thing to most men, but a revelation to be revealed to all man's understanding. This is not saying that Christ was the Father's first creation, but that the Son of God is the first begotten of the Father before he came into this world. The thought of Jesus would be created before Adams's creation; he was predestined before the foundation of the world (Rom. 8:29). The beginning of the creation of God is where Christ's destiny began.

What was Christ's destiny? To become the Lamb of God and the Resurrection and the Life. To become the Lion of the tribe of Judah, the Root of David, the Good Shephard, the Chief Shepherd, the Door, the Captain of our salvation, the Bishop of our souls, advocate, author and finisher of our faith, bread of life, corner stone, counselor, deliverer, the desire of all nations, a faithful witness, the glory of the Lord, head of the church, heir of all things, our Passover, prince of kings, life, peace, and redeemer. All these things were Christ's destiny for the sake of mankind. If Christ was from the beginning, if he was thought of before Adam were created, then death was coming before the tree of the knowledge and good and evil was placed in the garden. Jesus' body was being prepared well before he entered earth (Heb. 10:5). If Christ was prepared for death, why are we not preparing our lives for eternal life?

We know in the preparation of eternal life that we're going to suffer in the flesh. But it pleases the Father for his creation to suffer (1 Peter 4:1; Is. 53:10). The death, sorrow, crying, tears in our eyes, the pain, all these things were coming before the world began. Amazingly, our heavenly Father could not see how filthy flesh would become. In Genesis 6:6 the Word says, "It repented the Lord that he made man and it grieved him in his heart," the wickedness of flesh was great and is great today. The filthiness of flesh is excessive and the uncleanliness is abundant. All flesh of today has become an abomination to God. All flesh will come to an end like the day of Noah. Destruction is coming whether we believe it or not.

God is all knowing, but because of God's holiness and that everything he creates is good He cannot look on sin. I believe that the Lord's heart was prepared for the physical death of his creation. When God created Adam, I believe he knew that man would sin and physical death would come upon man, but he could not imagine what the spiritual death of his creation looked like. I believe he knew that man was going to sin through the tempting of Satan. However, I believe that God didn't know how great of a hurt he would experience from the disconnection of his creation.

God saw only one way for his creation to be redeemed. Christ, by the grace of God, should taste death for every man (Heb. 2:9-10). Christ had to taste physical death (John 19:30-34) for man. The blood of Christ is the redemption to show he is the Lamb of God who came in the likeness of sinful flesh. About the ninth hour Jesus cried with a loud voice (Matt. 27:46) showing that the sin and death of man was upon the perfect Lamb of God. From the very beginning God always had a sacrifice for the sin of man. God sacrificed the beast to make coats of skin to cover their nakedness (Gen. 3:21). In the book of Leviticus the Lord implemented the blood sacrifice of animals for the covering of sin; unfortunately those sacrifices were imperfect and could not take away sin completely.

Man must understand that sin and death can separate you from God the Father (Is. 59:2). Man looks at sin as something that God will overlook, but he's true to his Word. Because of the grace of Jesus Christ, God allows room for repentance because if he marked sin no one would stand (Ps. 130:3). God doesn't want servants that are dead, but he wants servants full of spiritual life for he is the God of the living not the dead (Matt. 22:32).

Many believers truly have no knowledge or understanding of what spiritual death is. Christ tasted spiritual darkness for three hours while he was upon the cross. Christ tasted spiritual condemnation for man, meaning, that at this time the Father showed strong disapproval of the sin that upon Christ. God passed sentence and judgment and declared Christ to be guilty of wrong-doing because of our sin. Christ tasted spiritual judgment from God; a judgment is sentence given by a judge, and God is the ultimate judge. Christ experienced dooms day; Christ tasted spiritual doom. He was rejected by God.

While Christ was on the cross there was darkness that was upon the earth for three hours, this was the same darkness that covered the universe before God said let there be light. This is that eternal darkness that Christ tasted and spoke about in Matthew 8:12. This darkness is what those who don't do the will of the Father will experience; you don't want to see, touch, taste, nor handle this darkness. You don't want to get beaten with any of these stripes of darkness.

To taste Christ's life we must taste the suffering and dying to this life. The suffering and death of the flesh separates you from this life of sin, but the reward is that you will be connected to Christ's life (Rom. 6:11). Christ tasted death to bring many sons into glory. Why do we need to become sons of God? We need to become sons because in the beginning the Father created sons (Gen 6:4).

In many passages of scriptures God referred to his holy angels as the sons of God. God's ultimate goal is to bring many sons unto glory (Heb. 2:10) - in the end we will be the angels of God (Matt. 22:30). We will be called sons of God because he gave us power to become like his Son (John 1:1). In the new heavens and new earth there will not be males and females. We will be like the angels; his sons of God. Christ dying for our sins on the cross and becoming sin is only for the benefit of the believer.

Bringing things back to Christ being the first born of every creature. The first born in a family is the child that is born first. Christ is the first born that came in the likeness of sinful flesh with a divine nature, heavenly nature, spiritual nature, and a sinless nature – Adam was missing the divine and heavenly nature.

Christ's divine nature: he was of God or like God; holy devoted to God. When the scripture says that Christ was the first born of every creature this means that everyone that was born again into the kingdom of Christ received that same divine nature that Christ came in. This means they are of God, like God, holy, and devoted to God.

Christ's heavenly nature: he was in a state or place of perfect union with God and eternal life. So if we're born into his kingdom we shall have a place in God and this place should be in perfect union with God and eternal life.

Christ and the church symbolize marriage: the husband and wife should be in perfect union with one another, no more twine but one – this is what perfect union with God means. We're one with him and not connected to any other thing that is in this world. If we connect ourselves with anything or anyone other than God then that union is broken; we are considered to be in spiritual adultery. The same as if a husband or wife have infidelity in the marriage which breaks the union vows of that marriage.

Christ's spiritual nature is his spiritual character. Jesus said except a man be born again (John 3:3) or become a new creature (2 Cor. 5:17) he cannot see the kingdom of

God. Jesus is the first born of every creature because every believer that is made alive spiritually in the inner man has become part of the kingdom of Christ – but, yet, walking in this earthly kingdom in a human body. Jesus is the first born of all the new creatures on earth.

Once the believer is born in the kingdom of Christ they can see and begin to understand how to live in Christ's kingdom on earth - and this is when their spiritual warfare begins.

What is spiritual warfare? Spiritual warfare is the fight between God and Christ's kingdom with Satan and his fallen angels that made war in heaven. Satan is not making war with the world because Satan is the god of that kingdom (the world). But according to the scriptures in Daniel 7:26-27 his kingdom is going to come to an end and the saints shall receive a kingdom that is an everlasting kingdom whose King is Christ and all dominion shall serve and obey him.

Christ is first born from the dead. Christ is the first person that rose from the dead and lived forever in a human body, meaning he is the first begotten from the dead, also. The definition of begotten[1] means to bring a child into existence by a father. Christ has a spiritual father and a God; he has a natural father and that father is Father

God the creator, who is also Christ's spiritual father because he came from God out of heaven. God is Christ's natural father because he impregnated Mary by the Holy Ghost. The reason that Joseph is not considered because he did not impregnate Mary in any way.

So he that hath an ear let him hear what the spirit says unto the churches (Rev. 2)… Christ is not speaking to the natural man when he compels man to hear, he is speaking to the inward man, the spirit of man. Many believers often believe they are *hearing* from the Lord, but how can they if their inward man is dead in trespasses and sins? If believers are walking in their own way and having their own thoughts, you tell me, how can they hear what the Spirit is saying?

Christ will never speak to your natural man's desires or wants. Christ has no parts of the flesh. Christ will always speak to the inward man, the spirit of man, but it must be alive and quickened in order to hear:

- Ephesians 1:1 – and you hath he quickened.
- John 4:24 – God is a spirit and they that worship him must worship him in spirit and in truth.
- Proverbs 20:27 – the spirit of man is the candle of the Lord searching all the inward parts of the belly

- Psalm 51:6 – behold thou desirest truth in the inward parts and in the hidden part thou shalt make me to know wisdom

But if the inward parts need to be washed and cleaned then how can your ear hear what the Spirit is saying to the church (Ps 51:2)? This I say then walk in the Spirit and ye shall not fulfil the lust of the flesh (Gal. 5:16) or walk in the Spirit and you will hear what the Spirit is saying to the church.

Can you hear? He that hath an ear let him hear what the spirit saith unto the churches. When we do hear from the Lord, many don't even understand or know who is talking to us - the Father, the Son, or the Holy Ghost. The Holy Ghost hears what Christ is saying to his Church and will deliver it to those that can hear him. God will never talk to you directly, he will always use the Holy Spirit. Many are deceived about this in this area.

> *Howbeit when he, the Spirit of truth, is come, he will guide you into all truth: for he shall not speak of himself; but whatsoever he shall hear that shall he speak: and he will shew you things to come. He shall glorify me; for he shall*

receive of mine, and shall shew it unto you.
John 16:13-14

I can hear what the Spirit is saying to the church today. He is saying that there is a great falling away. Now the Spirit speaks expressly, that in the latter times some shall depart from the faith (1 Tim. 4:1): and fall from the grace of God and the root of bitterness is springing up in many and defiled them (Heb. 12:15). I can hear the Holy Ghost say into my hearing, "Take heed brethren, lest there be in any of you an evil heart of unbelief in departing from the living God. But exhort one another daily, while it is called today; lest any of you be hardened through the deceitfulness of sin. For we are made partakers of Christ, if we hold the beginning of our confidence steadfast unto the end" (Heb. 3:12-13).

Because of the compelling of the Holy Ghost, I'm determined to live by the faith of the Son of God, who loved me, and gave himself for me. I'm afraid that in 2016 there is a door that is being opened and a door that is being shut.

And they that were ready went in with him to the marriage: and the door was shut. - Matthew 25:10

And they that went in, went in male and female of all flesh, as God had commanded him: and the Lord shut him in. - Genesis 7:16

Adam and Eve were shut into everlasting physical life and everlasting spiritual life until Adam ate from the tree of the knowledge of good and evil. Adam's disobedience opened the door to physical death, spiritual death, and eternal death. All mankind that is born of a mother will experience at least two of these deaths – and if they are not quickened from their sins and die without the Lord they will experience eternal death. David said in Psalm 51:5 that we were all shaped in iniquity and in sin our mother's conceived us.

Jesus said to Nicodemus that except a man be born of water and of the Spirit, he cannot enter into the Kingdom of God (John 3:3). I know I've said this in early chapters, but we must understand the importance of knowing that we will experience death if we are not alive in the spirit.

The scripture shows us that God shut the door to every angel that sinned and fell, and that they were casted out of heaven. Only those born of a natural, earthly body who is born again shall enter into the Kingdom of God. Jesus opened the Father's doors for the believer, but if they don't hear his voice they won't be able to enter in (John 5:24-25).

After death then there's judgment, this shuts the door to physical life on earth and opens two doors of eternity: you choose either heaven or hell. Sadly, many will chose the door of hell. In their mind they believe they are choosing the door of heaven but because of their deafness they will be choosing the door of hell.

> *If my people, which are called by my name,*
> *shall humble themselves, and pray, and seek*
> *my face and turn from their wicked ways...*
> 2 Chronicles 7:14

Are these the days that there is a famine in the congregation of hearing the Word of God, which the Lord promised to send (Amos 8:11)? Is the congregation unable to understand the parables in which the Lord speaks (Matt. 13:10-17)? I see deafness in the ears of the congregation.

Many believers in the congregations cannot hear what the Spirit is saying to the churches. The scripture is being fulfilled in our ears, the congregations cannot see, hear, nor understand. There is only a remnant that can see, hear, and understand – are you a part of this remnant?

Chapter 7
THE BODY & THE CANDLESTICK

He that hath an ear let him hear – this can't be said enough. God is begging the church to hear. There's a body in the church that doesn't have a head, there's a candlestick in the church that doesn't have a light.

The candlestick is the spirit of Christ that dwells in the born again believer, who is baptized into the body of Christ. The candlestick gives light to the believer that comes from Christ's light. The candlestick is the spirit of Christ, if man has not the spirit Christ; he is none of his (Rom. 8:9). The spirit of man cannot give light on its own, before Christ quickens you and makes the believer alive he is full of darkness. The sinner, whom is dead in trespass and sin, is incapable of producing light. Christ delivered him from the power of darkness and translated him into the body of Christ so the Lord could see his light. The Lord will never be able to see his life in a sinner or the ungodly because the Lord is light and in him there's no darkness at all. So if we say that we have fellowship with him and walk in darkness we lie and do not the truth (1 John 1:5-6).

Walking in darkness means to walk in the lust of *the spirit* of this world; to walk in the lust for *the things* of this world. I am not saying we can't have things but it's the lust for the things that does not please God. Lust is evil desires, unhealthy bodily appetites, over-mastering desires, intense desires, which is strong desires. But if we seek ye first the kingdom of God and his righteousness all these other things shall be added (Matt. 6:33).

Remember the light that comes from the believer, who is the candle, is Christ's light. Christ's light is to give us light to search all the inward parts of our belly, meaning our hearts. Our hearts are deceitful above all things and desperately wicked. Who can know the heart but God? David understood this and cried out to God saying, search me oh, God, and know my heart (Psalm 139:23-24). David could not search himself and know his heart; he could not know his thoughts because his candle (light) went out.

The candlestick that gives light comes from Christ's light because Christ is the light of the world – and ye are the light of the world. Neither do men light a candle and put it under a bush, but on a candlestick for all that are in the house (Matt. 5:15).

There's a candlestick in the church that don't have a light. There is no light in the candlestick or the church because the ministers have put out Christ's light. If there's no light in the candlestick and the ministers put this light out then this means there's no light in the temple of God.

Examples of ministers putting the light out in the temple:
1. By adding to the scriptures and taking away from them.
2. Using the scriptures for their own gain and for filthy lucre.
3. Preaching and teaching from their intellect without the Spirit of God. Using their fleshly knowledge to produce false revelation to deceive those that believe in the scriptures, but their revelation doesn't come from above. That's why Jesus said to Peter, when it was revealed to him that Jesus was the Son of the living God, that flesh and blood didn't reveal this but my Father which is in heaven.
4. The minister not having a light in his temple which is the spirit of God. When the minister has the Spirit of God in him, his preaching and teaching

will be reflective of reproving the world of sin, righteousness, and judgment. Examples of the sin that the preacher should be speaking out against is infidelity, fornication, idolatry, to name a few.

If there's no light in the temple of God, then many are sleep and in spiritual darkness. It's a mystery that some who are walking in the light are remaining in the temples that have no light. God commands those that are in the light to come out from among them and be ye separated. The Lord also commands the believer who walks in the light to touch no unclean things, so that he can receive you and you can be his sons and daughters (2 Cor. 6:17). Don't forget the scripture says touch not, taste not, and handle not unclean things. You know it's not good for a man to touch a woman to avoid fornication and vice versa – so let every man have his own wife and wife her own husband. Examine yourself child of God.

If Christ is the head then his power should be in his body; the power is expected to be in the body of Christ (Luke 10:19). If he is the head then his faith should be in the body. (Gal. 2:20). If he is the head then his love should be in the body. (John 13:35). If he is the head then his patience should be in the body (Rev. 3:10). If he is the head then his peace should be in the body (John 14:27). If he is the head then his life should be in the body (Col. 3:4). If he is the head then his strength should be in the body (Rev. 3:2).

Many churches today don't see themselves as a candlestick, this is why spiritual darkness is there (Luke 11:35-36). The Devil has blinded their minds to knowing and accepting that they should be candlesticks of the Lord; they don't see Jesus in the midst of them. If Jesus isn't there in the church then that means they are not his candlestick. And if they believe they are his candlestick and have not repented, then they cannot see The Lord has removed them out of their place. The church cannot see that they are no longer a part of the body of Christ.

Paul said in Rom 11:17 that some of the branches (believers) were broken off because of unbelief. The branches didn't see that if God spared not the natural branches that he would not spare the other branches because of their sins and unbelief. Paul exhorts us to take heed lest God also spare us not. Jesus said in Luke 13:3, "I tell you, nay but, except ye repent, ye shall all likewise perish" because of the darkness that dwelled in the church.

Today many cannot see that repentance will open up heaven's gates. Part of the reason they cannot see it is because they believe heaven's gates are already opened unto them. The church of Christ does not recognize the need to be renewed with spiritual blessings in heavenly places in Christ Jesus. The church is looking for spiritual blessings, but the blessings they're looking for are blessings that will please the flesh and not build up the body, the candlestick, the inner man.

The branches of the Lord are being broken off so that those that *will* hear, see, and understand may be grafted into God's kingdom. Jesus said I am the true vine, ye are the branches. Herein is my Father glorified, that ye bear much fruit; so shall ye be my disciples (John 15:5;8).

When you think about man being made in God's image, his images is not that of a natural human being, but of the perfect reflection of who his is. God's image has nothing to do with my physical appearance, but with my spiritual being (spirit, soul, and body).

My spirit should reflect God.

My body should reflect Jesus.

My soul should reflect the Holy Spirit.

When you pray, don't pray with an image of what God looks like. You are not praying to God if you envision a "human being figure" God, or if you envision him as an image. You have to pray in the Holy Ghost to connect with

God. You have to see God as spirit. You must see the Spirit that searches your heart, the only one who knows the mind of the Spirit and makes intercession for you (Rom. 8:26-27).

You will know if you're reflecting God's image when you begin to produce fruit. Jesus told us how we know when we're bearing fruit.

- Ye bear much fruit so shall you be my disciples (John 15:8): when you bear the fruit of Jesus then you are his disciples.
- If you continue in my word then are ye my disciples indeed (John 8:31): meaning obey the Word of God so that he will know you are his disciples.
- Whosoever do not bear his cross and come after me cannot be my disciples (Luke 14:27): meaning if you won't do it and you cannot do it you are not Christ's disciple.
- Whosoever he be of you that forsake not all, all that he have he cannot be my disciples (Luke 14:33): meaning lovers of pleasure more than lovers of God could never be Christ's disciple.
- Why call ye me, Lord, Lord, and do not the things which I say (Luke 6:46): meaning it is easy to

confess the Lord, but not easy to keep his commandments. Only those who keep the commandments of the Lord can be his disciple.
- Whoseover do the will of my Father which is in heaven, the same is my brother and sister and mother (Matt. 12:50): meaning if you know Jesus you will do the Father's will, you are now the family of Christ.

Before you consider yourself the body of Christ and the candlestick of the Lord, examine your life to see if it's reflective of God's true image. Are you bearing the fruit that Christ requires of thee? Are you truly prepared for the true celebration in the air?

Chapter 8
THE CELEBRATION IN THE AIR

Not only is there hidden pieces that are now revealed; but also there is a missing piece that will be revealed at the last day. The missing mystery is the Bride of Christ.

Revelation 19:7 says, "Let us be glad and rejoice, and give honour to him: for the marriage of the Lamb is come, and his wife hath made herself ready."

Remember those that were ready went in with him to the Marriage; and the door was shut and they were caught up in the clouds to meet the Lord in the air (1 Thess. 4:17).

Have you heard about the celebration in the air? Are you invited? Do you realize you need to be counted worthy to obtain this? It is false teaching to believe that everyone will make it to heaven. It is false teaching to believe that you don't have to be holy to be invited to the celebration in the air. It is false teaching that grace alone will save you and that once saved, always saved. Only he that do the will of the Father and walk in true holiness shall see God.

The cloud that will reveal the Bride of Christ will be a holy cloud. This cloud will possess all that is righteous and holy before the Lord. Although, I have not personally experienced this celebration I can only give you an idea of what it will be like when the saints are caught up in the air. Thomas said in John 20:27, "My Lord, my God", when he saw Christ in all his glory upon reaching hither his finger and beholding Christ's hands and thrusted his hand into Christ's side. Because of the glory that will be in the cloud, I believe we will proclaim the same statement as Thomas, "My Lord, my God." We will be in awe of the majesty of Christ.

Once we are caught up in the cloud we (the saints) are going to honor and recognize who God really is in his pure form. We will see that he is the Christ, the Son of the living God; the Resurrection and the Life. We will see our Redeemer living; the Holy Lamb of God! Which was slain, worthy to receive power and riches; wisdom and strength; honor and glory, and blessings.

In this cloud is Christ's glory, this is the glory that he had with the Father before the world began (John 17:5). In the high and holy mountain the Father spoke to Jesus in this, or out of this, glory. For when the disciples heard this voice out of this cloud, they fell on their faces and were sore afraid (Matt. 17:5-7).

The saints will be able to rejoice that we escaped the wrath of God; "for God hath not appointed us to wrath, but to obtain salvation by our Lord Jesus Christ" (1 Thess. 5:9). Those that didn't keep the commandments of the Lord will experience the wrath of God. What wrath? The wrath they will experience is a wrath of condemnation, judgement and the resurrection to damnation. This is the wrath that is not appointed to the saints of the most high.

When the cloud covers the saints in the air, those left on the earth shall hear a great noise. But they won't know that it's the joyful noise of the saints realizing that they have stepped into the glory of Christ.

What noise? What Peter said when the Father revealed to Peter who Christ was, "thou are the Christ the son of the living God."

What noise? What Thomas said to Christ, "again, how can we know the way? To which Jesus replied, I am the way the truth and the life."

What noise? What Phillip said to Christ, "Show us the Father and Jesus said to him, if you have seen me you have seen the Father."

What noise? When Isaiah saw Christ, he called him Wonderful, Counselor, the mighty God, the everlasting Father, Prince of Peace.

I ask you again, have you heard about the celebration in the air? Are you invited? What matter of love have the Father bestowed upon us that we shall be called sons of God? It does not yet appear what we shall be, but when he shall appear we shall be like him, as he is. This would be a celebration that the world will miss. Have you, as his bride, made yourself ready?

Chapter 9
WHY HAS GOD GIVEN ME THIS BOOK TO WRITE?

I've been asked why God gave me this book to write. Just like the scriptures were given to the apostles by inspiration of the Holy Spirit to edify the body of Christ, God gave me this book by the same inspiration. God has revealed to me secret things concerning the scriptures and events that have happened before this creation.

How are the saints supposed to use this book? I encourage the saints to use this book to build up their spiritual man that they may be able to overcome Satan's army and the deception that is in the world. God's will is that you be able to discern the spirit of truth and error.

Through my suffering in the wilderness, God discovered that he could trust me with his Holy Word and Holy Revelations; then I was charged with edifying his church through the writing of this book. He will, and is getting, the glory and honor and praise.

The Lord said, "I am the Lord: that is my name and my glory will I not give to another, neither my praise to graven images" (Is. 42:8). God led me in the wilderness and chose me for the furnace of affliction to walk through the fire. This wilderness and furnace of fire I experienced for many years. I remember continually searching for the understanding for years of why the Lord chose me for this life of suffering. I can remember asking the Lord, "why and how long wilt thou hide thy face from me? How long shall I take counsel in my soul, having sorrow in my heart daily, how long shall mine enemy be exalted over me" (Psalm 13:2).

The Lord revealed to me that at this time I was given a messenger of Satan to buffet me. The suffering that I was experiencing, I did not know that the Lord was birthing many revelations in me to write this book. Through this wilderness I was very surprised to see the wretchedness in me. A branch that needed a true vine (John 15:1). A bottle that needed new wine (Luke 5:38).

Now I can see that I could not be that fitted vessel that the Lord desired me to be without using the wilderness for suffering. The degree of suffering showed the Lord the things in me. My willingness to stay in the suffering and endure the wilderness showed the Lord that I was trustworthy. This showed the Lord that I could be a man after his own heart and that I could be his man, the vessel he would use to cry loud and spare not.

The suffering that I experienced in this wilderness was very fearful to me. You must ask why, but at the same time you may understand. I was worried about keeping my integrity and maintaining his ways before him. Remember, Father God said that Jesus was his beloved Son, in whom he was well pleased. My deepest desire in that wilderness was to please the Lord. Can you imagine that if it pleased the Lord to bruise Christ, how much more did it please him to bruise me? Especially if the bruising and destruction of my flesh would bring him glory and carry out his will on earth.

The experience that I had with the spirit world, meaning Satan and his kingdom, was something that I could have never imagined. I witnessed how some of my thoughts become a prey for Satan and his kingdom to use to gain advantage over me. I remember during my suffering I would talk to myself and think within myself. They would often speak to me to try and stop what I wanted to do in the Lord and change my mind of the things that I wanted to do for the Lord. Many times the demonic forces would transform themselves as an angel of light to deceive me. They wanted me to walk in their will and believe what they said, instead of trusting in the Word of God.

They wanted to possess me and fought me very hard to be in control. The Lord allowed this door to be opened in my life for many years. He allowed me to experience the testing of the Devil; through this suffering the eyes of my understanding have been enlightened.

I recognized that these spirits are liars, and through their lies their main focus was to convince me that their lies were the truth. Through the removing of God's hedge, the longer these spirits stay in your life the more they get to know you, and through suffering you get to know them. If you trust God's plan and stay rooted in the Word you will get to the point where they no longer will have an advantage over you. All of their lies, deceptive practices, and ungodliness will be revealed to you, it will no longer be hidden from you. You will be able to recognize the Devil afar off.

In the suffering, it felt like they were wearing me out. I become ignorant, at times, and didn't know what to do. It seemed like the Lord's weapons were no longer working for me. The defeat I thought I was experiencing made me believe that I was without God and without Christ in the spiritual warfare. I had to come to an understanding that the evil spirits had permission to do what they were doing, but also I gained an understanding that it was some things that God would not allow. Just like with the trying of Job, God had limitations of what Satan was allowed to do to Job. It was all for the building of my faith, my knowledge of Satan and his kingdom, and the power of God.

I'm glorying to report that the false and evil spirits do not have advantage over me like they did when I was in that spiritual darkness. I remember the anguish I would feel in believing that I had done something wrong that I didn't know about; feeling like the Lord was punishing me for the wrong. I can say the Lord strength is greater and his right hand of righteousness can uphold.

Even now, there are times when I call on him that he might not answer me, and many times during my wilderness he did not answer me when I called on him. However, at the end I know he was there. He would even let me know he was there. I cannot explain how he let me know that he is there with me – but something within my spirit let me know he was there. It's a true saying of the Word of God that he will never leave thee, nor forsake thee. Maybe the faith came from what I knew to be true in the Word of God.

Know that, *"the trial of your faith, being much more precious than of gold that perisheth, though it be tried with fire, might be found unto praise and honour and glory at the appearing of Jesus Christ"* (1Pet. 1:7).

There were many hidden pieces in this walk, but they have now been revealed. Know that God will use many avenues to ensure that you will be inexcusable, O, man (Rom. 2:1). The Lord is never slack concerning his promises toward this world. Some consider his delay as slackness, but truthfully he is extending grace to us because he is not willing that any should perish – his desire is that the world comes into repentance (2 Pet. 3:9). However, his spirit will not always strive with man (Gen. 6:3), judgement is soon to come be sure that that day come not upon you unaware (Luke 21:34).

JOHNNIE G. REDMOND

NOTES

Chapter 1: HIDDEN PIECES

1. *Deep: Webster's New World College Dictionary*, Houghton Mifflin Harcourt
2. *Condemn: Webster's New World College Dictionary*, Houghton Mifflin Harcourt
3. *Judgment: Webster's New World College Dictionary*, Houghton Mifflin Harcourt

Chapter 5: THE LITTLE BOOK

1. *Science:* www.yourdictionary.com
2. *Biology:* www.yourdictionary.com
3. *History:* www.yourdictionary.com

Chapter 6: JESUS THE BEGINNING OF THE CREATION

1. *Begotten:* www.yourdictionary.com

www.ingramcontent.com/pod-product-compliance
Lightning Source LLC
Chambersburg PA
CBHW070313100426
42743CB00011B/2442